THE Lazy Man's Hustle

Rate on Goodreads.com

Thank you Jerry!

1

Printed in the United States of America

First Printing, 2016

ISBN 978-1541016057

Ultra Diesel Time Publishing
Address not Disclosed

Contact the author at Phone number 571-295-4316

The

Lazy Man's

Hustle

THE Lazy Man's Hustle

Ultra Diesel Time

Rule No.1: Never lose money.

Rule No.2: Never forget rule No.1.

-Warren Buffett

THE LAZY MAN'S HUSTLE

By Durrell Hearns

THE Lazy Man's Hustle

Note from the author: Hello beautiful reader, my name is Durrell Hearns. I made this book for the person who is tired of the daily grind. I was in the same predicament years ago, then I left to pursue greater things. I was working and stacking to get myself off the plantation/9 to5. When I was at work I would catch myself daydreaming and seeing myself doing great things.

I love people. I have helped multiple people with my resources. I have helped people get books to pursue their future endeavors. Then give them advice.

I want the beautiful person reading this book to see how important it is to help people when you're up and how to get up. When they see themselves in the mirror, I want them to see success.

I double spaced the book so you can take notes in the book. I used to be a pastor in training. I hated having to draw lines to each thing I wanted to make note of.

I want this beautiful person reading this book to recommend this book to any friend or associate in a bad predicament. Then have them also pay it forward.

Thank you for your time!

THE Lazy Man's Hustle

THE LAZY MAN'S HUSTLE

Table of Contents

THE Lazy Man's Hustle

THE Lazy Man's Hustle

Intro to The Lazy Man's Hustle!

Do you want money but don't want to deal with overbearing bosses or backstabbing associates? Do you suffer from never having enough time in the day? Do you like to lay on the couch all day and watch TV but know you need money to keep the TV on? Then <u>The Lazy Man's Hustle</u> is for you. <u>The Lazy Man's Hustle</u> will keep money in your pocket with minimal effort. If done properly you can improve your life. Hello, my name is Durrell Hearns and I have been using <u>The Lazy Man's Hustle</u> for years. The <u>Lazy Man's Hustle</u> has made it possible for me to keep money in my pocket, with minim al effort, and look good doing it. I have worked the 9 to 5s and the 12 to 12s. All I did was lose money and become miserable. I was trying to impress millions of people but not considering my own value. Those same people would call me stupid because I wasn't trained properly. When I was let go from the job. The Lazy Man's Hustle made it possible for me to live off 2,000 dollars for two years. Never having to touch my savings account, out of necessity.

When I was working for a master I figured out I would die and leave my kids nothing because I wanted a master. I was making the master rich and not being recognized for any of it or better yet compensated properly.

I would ask for a raise and They would laugh in my face and talk about the benefits I received were worth more than the paycheck. I Disagreed.

In this book, I will teach you the smart money method and will teach the ways of <u>The Lazy Man's Hustle</u>. **The Master system for the Master's Master!**

Rules of the Lazy Man's Hustle

1. Find Yourself

2. Practice Self-Discipline

3.Make More with Less risk

4.Know you are the most important person in your life.

THE Lazy Man's Hustle

Chapter 1: What is the Lazy Man's Hustle?

The Lazy Man's Hustle is a system of keeping money in your pocket while enjoying your life. The Lazy Hustler doesn't need society to tell them they are lazy. The Lazy Hustler knows they are not lazy or lack motivation. They want to get by like the rest of world.

I'm not here to give you throw away motivational quotes. Any person can say "The hat doesn't get itself. You get the hat." or any other "malarkey quotes". While they are in t he same position (at a job they hate) for 50 years. That's time that could be used watching a video on YouTube, a new video game, or your future endeavors. We are not made to work 200-hour work weeks (possibly weekends) For a job that will fire us if we don't kiss enough ass. The Lazy Man's Hustle keeps you from a life of failure.

Using The Lazy Man's Hustle properly you can become rich enough to slap your old boss in the face. (Not that I condone that) The Lazy Man's hustle involves the communion with Smart Money. Smart Money works for you and your goals while handling the immediate threats. "What are the immediate threats?" you ask. The immediate threats are Bills and Life's unexpected (which this book will show you how to keep them in check). Bills are those things that come to you on a monthly basis. You can't keep them piled up in the corner making yourself a new sofa. You must pay them eventually.

Life's unexpected is anything that comes up out of nowhere (which can be surprise bills). They range from a visit to the emergency room to a dying loved one. You need money for both of those. Especially if you plan on having good credit. Which this book covers.

The Lazy Man's Hustle is the answer to those who call you lethargic. The ones who tell you to get a job. When your bank account looks better than theirs, and you are handling business. Those are the same people that tell you the way of the world is the answer. You can live comfortably knowing these people are but peasants to royalty.

I learned years ago, that you only listen to the winners. I have been listening to the winners for years and have saved a great deal of money doing so. Because I don't invest in people's failed experiments like drug addiction and materialism. I have lost dozens of friends because my pockets aren't for them. They will tug at your heartstrings and tell you that you are a failure as a person for not supporting their h abits. Remember, this is coming from someone asking you for help. They don't know what power feels like.

The Lazy Man's Hustle is not for the people run by th e world. The world will tell you are a failure for not living up to its standards and that you are wasting your time on the planet. Remember, these are the people who are not ready for the future and live outside their means without actual a ssets. Their assets are for impressing people who will forge t them when they are in a slump. Your assets are for your c hildren's, children's, children.

THE Lazy Man's Hustle

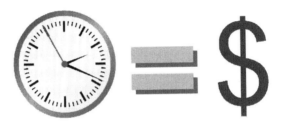

Chapter 2: Your Time is Valuable!!

Have you been at work and caught yourself day dreaming? Did you see yourself outside enjoying life with your family or friends? Did you see yourself owning a flourishing business? Have you wanted to celebrate a holiday but your job wouldn't let you? (Or my favorite) Having a family member die and you must jump through hoops to go to the funeral for them. Your life and time on this planet is valuable. People may pay you for your time, but You and I both know it's worth more than 1.00 an hour.

You need to put value in yourself and your time. Time is your contribution to this world. You should make the most out of it. We are put here to make a change to this beautiful planet. We may not know our purpose when we get to this world but we find out, once we know ourselves. This takes focusing on YOUR goals and no one else's, or you may find yourself in another person's shadow. You must go back to when you were a kid with an imagination. What did you think about? (give yourself a minute)

I put myself in this mind state when I hear myself complain about my job or when a boss tells me "he does his job because he has to pay a high mortgage." I tell myself to remember my dreams I had and go for them. Because I don't want to die with regrets.

I know too many people who died with regrets. They wanted to be in that movie, but nobody would hire them. They wanted to be an author, but didn't know where to start. I f you are alive (even if you are "lazy") you can add somethin g of value to your life. Which if you're like me, you value mo ney.

I was in the worst spot in my early 20s. I joined the military without a plan. I was in basic training being set up by shitty people with high school mindsets. I was told to do most of everything and was treated like a slave. The teachi ngs I would receive from my supervisors were reactionary. Nobody cared about anyone but their selves. I must have w atched too many movies, because I thought the military wa s about brotherhood. Most competed in the off-duty life for the best dressed slave.

I was working 12 hour shifts every day. This was mo st of my time on this world taken. I was around some of the most venomous of people. They made me feel depressed a nd dead inside. Most of them were but they dealt with it by becoming bullies. This made it feel like I was throwing my life away for 15 dollars a day plus "benefits"

This had so much bearing on my life. I was into music and had multiple hobbies that couldn't wait for the occasional weekend or holiday. Because I needed to sleep for the next 12-hour shift. They would tell me it's about time management. This was their way of saying fuck you. I was blessed to get out with my twenties intact. Some let themselves get drained to the point of suicide. Luckily, I never pondered suicide because I played smart money and barely hung out with anybody with negative energy. My time and my money went hand in hand and kept me company.

I wasn't building anything with that job for my kids but a pension that would lose value with inflation. My kids would have to pay for my funeral and not have anything left over for themselves. This would be a viscous cycle that would never stop.

I would have been a fart in the world. A quick stench that dissipates. My claim to success would be, being fit enough to sign papers.

My time was wasted because I wanted to be coddled by a shitty world. Moral is, it's your time you should be able to use it anyway you want. You shouldn't have to ask people for your time off. If you invest all your time into yourself. Who do you ask to leave early? You? I had a family member die while I was in the military. I had to jump through hoops just to be told I was not allowed to go to their funeral. If I was invested in myself. I wouldn't have to ask for anything.

Or maybe, you get that sinking feeling from calling in sick from work. You shouldn't have to call anybody if you are sick. Your body doesn't want you to go to work! Your supervisor can say yes or no to you. I hate it when other people control my time and my body. I'm sure everyone does. It

THE Lazy Man's Hustle

makes you feel powerless. You feel like you are asking God for a day to be sick. Just to be told no.

Let's make the most of our short time here. I was taught about time management at a young age. I have a better way of doing this. It's called Multitasking. Multitasking is the art of doing multiple task at once. I love to be entertained and informed. I keep YouTube in the background of everything. It helps me focus on my important task. I know people that use Netflix or music. I also make notes to follow my projects. I call it an outline. The outline keeps me focused on the task.

I keep my outline in a notebook to keep me on my journey. There are times we will be discouraged or distracted by dooky or dooky people. The outline I use is basic and accessible to anyone.

For my outline, I put the goal as the title on the very top of the page. It helps me remember what project I am w orking on. I know we all have busy lives so as soon as we lo ok away from a project we may lose track of which project we are working on.

Next I do bullet points. Dates and progress can be a dded to this list. I see when and where I want to be to work on a certain project. The bullet names should be deadly. Yo u must feel what you want your people want to feel. You co uld use a dull name for your points but what makes you wa nt to work on them. My system is using epic names becaus e if you're not your number one fan...who is?

My gym time is called "the climb to strength" but I'm usually running. I feel this is a climb to strength because I b ecome stronger and better every visit. It helps if you leave y ourself notes of encouragement for everything on your list. Tell yourself how good of a person you are, How you improv ed today, and how you changed a person's life for the bette r. You did this nobody else. You should be proud of yourself. You will brighten your own day even if people try to ruin it. Which they will try their hardest.

I also add sub bullets to my outline. I put what I will be doing that day, How I will be doing it, and why I am doin g it. The world is a mysterious place. We only know a quart er of it. It helps if you know why you are doing certain thing s. The sub bullets can become bullets if you feel they are m ore important. You have the power and that's what it's all a bout

The bullets need levels. The outline guides your day and helps with your sense of accomplishment. This means you must know what is important to you and what time you want to do it. The most pressing thing for me is being healt hier. If I could say a goal. The top of my outline tells me you need a healthy breakfast this morning. The note says "Have a good day!" with this I am sending myself positive energy t hrough text. I can get through my day happy and more focu sed on my goals.

Finding your purpose in life is very important becaus e it keeps the BS away. It keeps you focused and ready for war. I say ready for war because life will not improve unless you make it change today. Every day you wake is a battle. T hink about improving a skill every day. You must have the t ools you need to do what is important. Because you can't h elp others while you are drowning.

Ways to value your time:

1. Focus on completing your goals
2. Find ways to better yourself

USE THIS FREE SPACE TO MAKE YOUR OUTLINE!

THE Lazy Man's Hustle

THE Lazy Man's Hustle

Chapter3: You like to chill? I do too!

All of us like to chill and be lazy. If that weren't true we wouldn't have spas, movie theatres, TV, books (like this one), or computers. We have all these things to take a load off ourselves from a busy day. If you ask at least five people (when their boss isn't around) would tell you that they hate their jobs. I tell you if there was a way to get people to make money without moving a muscle. Millions of people would do it. I'm on that list. It's taken a lot out of me to make this life cheat book. I usually sit on the couch all day and maybe if the sun is right in the sky. I will move a muscle. I make good money doing lazy man hustles like, making videos, selling things, and a podcast. Minimal effort stuff.

I have learned how to do these types of things laying in my bed and watching videos. There are so many videos online that teach you how to do just about anything, FOR FREE! I learned how to write a book, how to program, how to box, and how to speak in front of a group. These are what we call skills. Skills can become resources. Resources help you sustain or improve your life and the lives of others.

You could teach these skills to people and become the best, richest, instructor in the world. You can be a consultant for a big business and tell them how much to pay you for your opinion. I like the idea of having people pay you to do seminars to better themselves and others.

Skills are a tool for you get more resources in your pocket. Everyone's favorite resources come in the form of money. Money makes things happen and keeps the poo-poo out of your life.

I have seen this in first person. There have been several times I have seen that a speeding ticket can become a warrant. Then a warrant can become JAIL TIME. Why do I want that in my life? There are too many things to experience in life and too much money to get. Why am I going to give my freedom to a prison? I (and you if you are reading this book) don't like being controlled.

My process for learning a new skill is to center myself and treat it how I would treat it if a boss told me to get the training. We overlook this feature in our life. If someone is telling you to do something (especially in a rough tone or paying you) we tend to take it seriously. We don't take our own task that serious because at a young

41

age we're told not to take anything serious unless it's life threatening. We should take everything we do in our life serious. Because this is our time on this planet and believe me its short.

The next step I take is to take notes of the important stuff. Most videos will have side comments from the presenter or things that have nothing to do with the skill you're trying to learn. I try to be an active lazy listener in the comfort of my home or the library. This includes playing back what I hear if I don't understand it. Then I search for what was meant to be said in google (or your preferred search engine). I have heard many a goofy video that made me laugh but never taught me a thing. I have had many a boring "professor in front of a board" type video, which I never learned from because I was sleep. In this situation, I use Discernment.

Discernment is key in any situation. It sets us apart from the followers. The follower follows any trash person with a smile and a tickle of the ear. A leader discerns from the garbage and follows their own path. They can tell when they are being swindled by a snake oil salesman. My point is to pick your videos wisely. Some people just want your views and never make a point. The point is to learn a skill, not be entertained. Entertainment is a waste of time to The Lazy Hustler!

What skills do you want to learn?

THE Lazy Man's Hustle

CHAPTER 4: LIVE Within your Means

Living within your means is the key point of The Lazy Man's Hustle. This means highlight this chapter in super deep red. One of the many ways to be free is not to put yourself in debt. I see so many people going to college and receiving their degrees but degrees never guarantee a job. This means the debt will come before the pay, if you are not smart. Most people get jobs in college but you're the lazy man practitioner. We get our money other ways without people harassing you.

"Living within your means" means you need to know where to cut corners. If you can't afford that new car with the coffee maker in the cup holder, don't get it. Money has many purposes and jobs. It can be a resource, a friend, a comforter, a healer, and a producer. Never turn your back on a good resource that you can't bring back. The good resource keeps you above water and gets rid of the B.S. Money can make you a power player that can influence the top/bottom people in the world. Money tells you how to spend it. If you listen to it.

Living within your means takes a lot of discipline. You must be able to tell yourself no. If your money is telling you not to buy a TV, don't. It's for good reason. There may be a better cause for your money down the road. Instead of getting a TV. You get the opportunity to invest in land for your future.

It may take a while to build it up but follow through. Have you ever had an idea for a product and you don't have the money for it? This is because your money opportunity cost took its toll on your life. You said that 20-dollar cover charge to get in the club was a great idea. Now, you're looking at a blown tire on the side of the road with no money to get a new one or call roadside assistance.

The necessities come first. We must keep our wants different from our needs. We need food and water to live. If we run out of water in our body. Our body seizes up. I would rather have water than a jug of gold. If I'm in a desert I don't want to carry ounces and ounces of gold on my body. I'll get a weird tan and get exhausted faster than the person that wanted water. I have always focused on my necessities first. My basic needs need to be met before I get anything extra.

Your means are the most important things in your life. your means are your comfort. They help you make decisions in life. The means justify your end. You want to be something in life? It takes money. You want to be a lifetime student? It takes money. I once wanted to be an astronauts/rapper. The microphone and years of schooling takes someone's lots of money (or you're doing something strange for some change). This leads me to the more cost effective certification

Certifications are a great way to stay within your means and achieve your goals. There are certifications for everything you can think of. I know people who became ordained ministers through the internet. This is frowned upon in the world, but you are not a part of the world. Think about something you really want to do. There are multiple credible institutes that will certify you in that, and

remember the money you just saved? You just paid the full

price and didn't have to start indentured servitude, I mean

payment plan. I don't want you to become a slave to debt.

<u>Freedom is what you want. The Lazy Man's Hustle is</u>

<u>here to provide.</u>

THE Lazy Man's Hustle

Chapter 5: Focus on Self

The key point of the Lazy Man's Hustle is to focus on yourself. The focus on yourself means what you need to do. Not what everyone else is doing. You need your money. Even if you have extra money left over. I'm not saying not to help your fellow man but if they want money they need to help you.

You reward good behavior. Good behavior is when people do things in your best interest. If you don't believe me. Fart in someone's face and tell me you're not doing something bad when they hit you. They hit you because your fart wasn't in their self-interest. It may have ruined their day. When people tell you to get up right now. You shouldn't because you know your goals, They Don't. You may have an important meeting about resources at 10pm.

My secret is that I take every rude interaction personally. I do this because it motivates me to improve my reaction/strategies. When someone tells me "you're nothing because your broke" I act broker. If somebody tells me "you have nothing going on in your life" I play dead. People will always project themselves on to you. You just play along until you have them in that snare. Work as a undercover cop on a big case. You make your target show the evidence. Sometimes you must plant it. To make them get a false comfort you nod your head and agree. Go with everything they say. They don't need to know your true intention. Your intention is your goal in the end.

Goals give life a point. Your goal is where you want to be, to have, to do, within a given time span. Therefore, in job interviews they ask you "where do you want to be in 5 years?" This is to make sure you are a good investment for them. You see how they put their goals above you? That's how you must be. You should treat every interaction with anybody as an investment. The investment is your goal with money. The Lazy Man may not have billions of dollars but he does have friends. The smart lazy man makes them work for them. Be it mental health, food, ride, or motivation. Yes, get your friends to get this book and get on the same page. Then you have an army. A militia if you will.

Then you make a mission statement. Then you have a corporation. Then comes the profit. The profit becomes resources. So on and so on. We have to recognize money isn't everything but everything needs money. You say you want to live in the woods? Do you know how to build a cabin? Do you know how to get light in your cabin? Well then you either need people to help you or the knowledge. Only way to get this is money.

Money can create opportunity. The opportunity in the cabin scenario is in the knowledge gained to build a great Cabin. Most use the internet for all knowledge gain even if it involves "top 10 90s cartoons". All jokes aside. The internet isn't going to be in the middle of nowhere. So, you could use a book. The book takes money. The library isn't going to always have your book (you also must give it back or suffer your credit being messed with). Make the book come to you by getting it for free.

Your goal is more important than any acceptance. Can acceptance pay your bills? Can acceptance free you from debt? Can acceptance keep you at peace or are you stuck trying to impress people you don't know? Some things that I noticed when acceptance is more important than resources is you lose more resources and have to beg the acceptors for resources. I know all of us need to be social but when validation is more important than life, you are messing up somewhere. We have movies out there where they tell people "being a good person with no money is more important than having money" no matter what in life, don't believe that. You can help more people with one billion resources than with zero resources. Helping 100s of people when you have money makes you influential.

If you notice, in this world you need to be influential. The most influential people in the world have money. They take the time to focus on themselves and build their skills. Either from a mentor or reading multiple books. They sacrificed time with friends to learn how to make money not make 2 dollars an hour. They found out what people want and deliver it to them personally.

Everything in life takes sacrifice but it's up to us to accept that sacrifice or let the opportunity go away. You are the most important person in your life. Give yourself a chance to succeed and take that DIVE!

What do you want to be selfish about?

THE Lazy Man's Hustle

Chapter 6: Ways to avoid debt

and Live Free!!

I have noticed in my life, people my age and older live in necessity. We either had too many drinks and got the wrong one pregnant. We didn't make the right plan or a bad choice, or we hang with the wrong group. I know most people are in debt from trying to Impress others or spending out of their means.

Every resource I receive I put at least 10% into savings or investments. This is what I call "paying yourself". I say you're paying yourself because it goes directly to you. You can use it for emergencies or that expensive investment you want to buy right out and piss your enemies off. This takes me to the investment part of the Lazy Man's Hustle.

You remember those people that told you to get a job for benefits. Well you can do that for yourself. You go to a bank and get an investment account that acts like a 401k. Ask for the specific for what kind of account works for you.

Use a different bank than the one you mainly use. You want your money in different places. Hacking is a big problem nowadays so you want to have some emergency money that wasn't touched by hackers. Keep a little money in your mattress to keep it away from dirty people who have become jealous of your money. You don't want the IRS touching your money either. But if you file your taxes yearly you should be ok.

There are multiple resources out there to help you get your taxes together. I get them done for free because it saves me money. Lazy Hustlers get 1099s not W2s.You don't have to use the tax people on TV. I used to use them all the time and all they did was take my money. I was paying for a service I could have gotten for free. I was disgusted with myself when I figured this out. I felt like I wasted a resource. I feel there's always a cheaper option.

There's always a cheaper option for anything you want. They are usually of a good quality too. You should do a price match of any product you find in the store. If you can't afford it then, check out **anywhere** else. It may be two cents off but its two cents towards your resources and future. If a product cuts into your money way too much.

Then don't get it. You can get a credit card but you should look at how much debt you will get into doing so.

Credit cards can be good for your credit score. A good trick with those is to put a low-cost recurring bill (8-9 dollars...a Netflix account) on a credit card and pay it monthly. This makes it look like you pay your bills on time. This makes your credit score go up a little. When you get a good credit score. You can buy a house or a car and pay a lower amount of interest monthly. I know people with 30,000 dollar cars and they pay 100 dollars monthly. This should come when you have a stable form of income. Not dealing with shitty people. This is smart money and apart of the Lazy Man's Hustle.

Smart money keeps itself strong. Smart money has a strategy for any situation. Smart money quantifies itself when it needs to for battle. If more people thought like smart money, we would have more entrepreneurs in the world. Smart money talks as a part of its strategy. The smartest money doesn't answer to anyone. If smart money doesn't want to come into work that day, it doesn't!

You can get fired and live comfortably for a year. Within that year, not feel depressed about losing a job, but moving on to the next endeavor. There are many alternatives that pay you for your time when you help them immediately. Apps, websites, so forth. You don't have to work a 9 to 5 contractually. I have used these apps when I want to make an extra 100 dollars in a day. I'll go out and do the job. Then put the 100 dollars in my account. This is where learning a trade comes in.

A trade is defined as a skilled job, requiring manual skills and special training. Let's say you are a plumber. A plumber gets paid for their services. (laying pipe) They usually work out of their homes and have tools with them. The tools are at most a tax write-off. This means all you're paying for is learning the skill and a license. At most this will cost you 400 dollars if you shop around. I bet you could find lower costing license's. being licensed, won't be as bad in the long run because you can work for yourself, when no one is hiring.

Those same people who aren't hiring will pay you twice as much to fix their toilet, run wire through their workplace, etc. You get to leave when the job is done and not worry about work beef. Those same non-hiring places will call you back eventually to pay you more to do another job. Then you can hire employees because of how good your money is. Then more money is going into your pocket.

What can you cut back on?

THE Lazy Man's Hustle

Conclusion to the Lazy Man's Hustle

The Lazy Man's Hustle is the answer to all money and mental health ails. It helps you believe in yourself and helps you move forward in life. I appreciate you for picking up my book and giving me 20 minutes of your life. Now go out and institute what you learned into your daily activities. I believe in you and now you believe in you. **MAKE IT HAPPEN**. The world is waiting for you to change it. Use what you learned from this book to make a difference in your life. Then improve the life of others. Follow your dreams and make your dream come to reality and flourish.

Thank you for your time.

THE Lazy Man's Hustle

Made in the USA
Middletown, DE
05 March 2017